C.S.LEWIS

~ on ~

JOY

C.S. LEWIS

~ *on* ~

JOY

Compiled by

LESLEY WALMSLEY

THOMAS NELSON PUBLISHERS
Nashville

Published in Nashville, Tennessee
by Thomas Nelson, Inc.

1 2 3 4 5 6 – 03 02 01 00 99 98

Produced for Thomas Nelson Inc. by Godsfield Press

Designed and produced by
THE BRIDGEWATER BOOK COMPANY LTD

Picture research by Jane Moore

The Catalog Card Number is on file
with the Library of Congress.

ISBN 0 7852 7097 3

Printed in Hong Kong

Contents

Introduction

'J oy' comes from the Latin word meaning 'to be glad', but over the years it has taken on a stronger sense of rapture, of being uplifted, and we can all recognize the feeling even if we don't experience it very often. We want that experience, long for it to come to us, even just sometimes in our life, and we search to recognize it in the lives of others.

For C.S. Lewis joy took on a special meaning, and in this selection from his writings I hope you will be able to catch those moments when it came to him. Although he never sat down to write about joy in quite the same way as he did about faith, in the autobiographical Surprised By Joy he tells how he was finally overtaken by joy and was reluctantly converted to belief in a loving God. In his other writings he records other moments of joy in such things as a simple toy made by his brother, in books, music, the countryside, friendship – the kinds of things that we can all enjoy when we stop to look for them. None of Jack Lewis's sources of joy requires material wealth, simply an open heart and a wealth of spirit.

Warnie in uniform, 1916

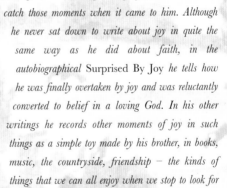

Clive Staples (Jack) Lewis was born in Belfast on 29 November 1898, the younger of two brothers brought up by their rather 'dry' father after their mother's early death. Their father did his best for them, but the Lewis home was probably not a very joyful one, and when the boys were sent to boarding school in England, Jack Lewis at least suffered miserably. His brother Warren

Arthur Greeves

(Warnie) was his rock and strength, both then and for the rest of his life. Jack also had a good friend in a neighbour at home, Arthur Greeves, whose company he enjoyed in the school vacations, and with whom he corresponded until his death in 1963.

Jack served for a time in the army during the First World War, but was invalided out and went to resume his studies at the university of Oxford. Here he was in his element, enjoying the companionship of lecturers and undergraduates alike in what was largely a masculine world. Several of his friends there were Christians, and he enjoyed the general stimulation of religious debate although he was by then an atheist, and felt no real threat

from their Christian arguments. But joy was there in the background and eventually, on 28 September 1931, Jack Lewis's conversion was complete and he became certain that Jesus Christ was the Son of God. From then on, although he continued his main work as lecturer in English (he had been elected a Fellow of Magdalen in 1925), Jack Lewis began the writings which were so to influence people throughout the world for the rest of the twentieth century, beginning with The Pilgrim's Regress *in 1932.*

C.S. Lewis

It was in 1952 that Lewis first met the woman he was later to marry, Helen Joy Davidman, an American writer with whom he had corresponded. In 1953 she returned to England with her two young sons. She was always known by her second name of Joy, and she was to bring a very special sort of joy to Lewis in their short married life.

Magdalen College,
Oxford

Jack Lewis was writing in a very different kind of world from the one in which we live today. In particular, as women were then only beginning to exert much influence outside the home, it was quite normal to refer to 'a man who', whereas today we would use more inclusive language. Lewis respected everyone for what they were, and if he were writing now I am sure that this would be reflected in his style. But he is not, and I have decided to leave his thoughts as he expressed them.

I hope that this selection of Lewis's thoughts on joy will help you find joy in your own life.

≈ *LESLEY WALMSLEY*

C.S. Lewis in his study at Magdalen College, 1947

The first beauty

This book *(Surprised By Joy)* is written partly in answer to requests that I would tell how I passed from atheism to Christianity... How far the story matters to anyone but myself depends on the degree to which others have experienced what I call 'joy'. If it is at all common, a more detailed treatment of it than has (I believe) been attempted before may be of some use. I have been emboldened to write of it because I notice that a man seldom mentions what he had supposed to be his most idiosyncratic sensations without receiving from at least one (often more) of those present the reply, 'What! Have *you* felt that too? I always thought I was the only one.'...

Jack and Warnie,
1949

Once in those very early days my brother brought into the nursery the lid of a biscuit tin which he had covered with moss and garnished with twigs and flowers so as to make it a toy garden or a toy forest. That was the first beauty I ever knew. What the real garden had

failed to do, the toy garden did. It made me aware of nature – not, indeed, as a storehouse of forms and colours but as something cool, dewy, fresh, exuberant. I do not think the impression was very important at the moment, but it soon became important in memory. As long as I live my imagination of Paradise will retain something of my brother's toy garden.

≈ *SURPRISED BY JOY*

In the Wood, ALFRED SISLEY (1839–99)

A world of happiness

I was, I believe, an intolerable chatterbox. But solitude was nearly always at my command, somewhere in the garden or somewhere in the house. I had now learned both to read and write; I had a dozen things to do.

What drove me to write was the extreme manual clumsiness from which I have always suffered... I longed to make things, ships, houses, engines. Many sheets of cardboard and pairs of scissors I spoiled, only to turn

from my hopeless failures in tears. As a last resort, as a *pis aller,* I was driven to write stories instead; little dreaming to what a world of happiness I was being admitted. You can do more with a castle in a story than with the best cardboard castle that ever stood on a nursery table.

I soon staked out a claim to one of the attics and made it 'my study'. Pictures, of my own making or cut from brightly coloured Christmas numbers of magazines, were nailed on the walls... Here my first stories were written, and illustrated, with enormous satisfaction. They were an attempt to combine my two chief literary pleasures – 'dressed animals' and 'knights-in-armour'... Then Animal-Land had to be geographically related to my brother's India... We made it an island, with its north coast running along the back of the Himalayas; between it and Animal-Land my brother rapidly invented the principal steamship routes. Soon there was a whole world and a map of that world which used every colour in my paintbox.

≈ *SURPRISED BY JOY*

The most faithful of friends

Arthur was the youngest son of a doting mother and a harsh father, two evils whereof each increased the other. The mother soothed him the more, to compensate for the father's harshness, and the father became harsher to counteract the ill effects of the mother's indulgence... It can be easily imagined how such a child grew up: but who could have foretold that he would be neither a liar nor a tale-bearer, neither a coward nor a misanthrope? He was the frankest of men. Many of the most ludicrous episodes which could be told against him turn on his failure to acquire that 'visor to the human face' which such a training usually teaches a man to wear. He was the most faithful of friends, and carried the innumerable secrets of my own furtive and ignoble adolescence locked in a silence which is not uncommonly thought effeminate...

Arthur Greeves

≈ *THEY STAND TOGETHER*

Even to an ecstasy

Until I met him, and during my frequent absences, his position was much the same as that of an imaginative boy in one of our public schools. Yet he never showed any inclination to revenge himself after the fashion so familiar among our modern intelligentsia. He continued to feel... at once a human affection and a rich aesthetic relish for his antedeluvian aunts, his mill-owning uncles, his mother's servants, the postman on our roads, and the cottagers whom we met in our walks. What he called the 'homely' was the natural food both of his heart and his imagination. A bright hearth seen through an open door as we passed, a train of ducks following a brawny farmer's wife, a drill of cabbages, in a suburban garden – these were things that never failed to move him, even to an ecstasy, and he never found them incompatible with his admiration for Proust, or Wyndham Lewis, or Picasso.

≈ *THEY STAND TOGETHER*

I call it Joy

(Animal-Land) was not imaginative. But certain other experiences were... The first is itself the memory of a memory. As I stood beside a flowering currant bush on a summer day there suddenly arose in me without warning, and as if from a depth not of years but of centuries, the memory of that earlier morning at the Old House when my brother had brought his toy garden into the nursery. It is difficult to find words strong enough for the sensation which came over me; Milton's 'enormous bliss' of Eden (giving the full, ancient meaning to 'enormous') comes somewhere near it. It was a sensation, of course, of desire; but desire for what?... Before I knew what I desired, the desire itself was gone, the whole glimpse... withdrawn, the world turned commonplace again, or only stirred by a longing for the longing that had just ceased...

In a sense the central story of my life is about nothing else... The quality common to the three experiences... is that of an unsatisfied desire which is itself more desirable than any other satisfaction. I call it Joy, which is here a technical term and must be sharply distinguished both from Happiness and Pleasure. Joy (in my sense) has indeed one characteristic, and one only, in common with them; the fact that anyone who has experienced it will want it again... I doubt whether anyone who has tasted it would ever, if both were in his power, exchange it for all the pleasures in the world. But then Joy is never in our power and Pleasure often is.

≈ *SURPRISED BY JOY*

The book is
a glorious feast

I have nearly finished *The Morte D'Arthur*. I am more pleased at having bought it every day, as it has opened up a new world to me. I had no idea that the Arthurian legends were so fine... Malory is really not a great author, but he has two excellent gifts, (1) that of lively narrative and (2) the power of getting you to know characters by gradual association... The very names of the chapters, as they spring to meet the eye, bear with them a fresh, sweet breath from the old-time, faery world, wherein the author moves...

What is nicer than to get a book – doubtful both about reading matter and edition, and then to find both are topping? By way of balancing my disappointment in *Tristan* I have just had this pleasure in Sidney's *Arcadia*. Oh, Arthur, you simply must get it... When you see the book yourself, you will be green with envy. To begin with, it is exactly the sort of edition you describe in your last letter – strong, plain, scholarly looking and delightfully – what shall I say – solid: that word doesn't really do, but I mean it is the exact opposite of the 'little

book' type we're beginning to get tired of. The paper is beautiful, and the type also.

The book itself is a glorious feast: I don't know how to explain its particular charm, because it is not like anything I ever read before: and yet in places like all of them... I am just longing for Saturday when I can plunge into it again.

≈ *THEY STAND TOGETHER*

A sudden intense
feeling of delight

What I feel like saying, if I am to give you my news, is 'Things are going very, very well with me (spiritually).' On the other hand, one knows from bitter experience that he who standeth should take heed lest he fall, and that anything remotely like pride is certain to bring an awful crash. The old doctrine is quite true you know – that one must attribute everything to the grace of God, and nothing to oneself... I seem to have been supported in respect to chastity and anger more continuously, and with less struggle, for the last ten days or so than I often remember to have been: and have had the most delicious moments of *It* (Joy). Indeed today – another of those days which I seem to have described so often lately, the same winter sunshine, the same gilt and grey skies shining through bare shock-headed bushes, the same restful pale ploughland and grass, and more than usual of the birds darting out their sudden, almost cruelly poignant songs – today I got such a sudden intense feeling of delight that it sort of stopped

Autumn, Kinnardy, JAMES McINTOSH PATRICK (B.1907)

me in my walk and spun me round. Indeed the
sweetness was so great, and seemed so to affect the
whole body as well as the mind, that it gave me pause –
it was so very like sex... However, one cannot be too
careful: one must try to hold fast to one's duties (I wish I
did) which are the prose of the spiritual life and not learn
to depend too much on these delightful moments.

≈ *THEY STAND TOGETHER*

By Lamplight, HARRIET BACKER (1845–1933)

On a Saturday afternoon in winter

Meanwhile, on afternoons and on Sundays, Surrey lay open to me. County Down in the holidays and Surrey in the term – it was an excellent contrast. Perhaps, since their beauties were such that even a fool could not force them into competition, this cured me once and for all of the pernicious tendency to compare and to prefer – an operation that does little good even when we are dealing with works of art, and endless harm

when we are dealing with nature. Total surrender is the first step towards the fruition of either. Shut your mouth; open your eyes and ears. Take in what there is and give no thought to what might have been there or what is somewhere else…

What delighted me in Surrey was its intricacy… The contours were so tortuous, the little valleys so narrow, there was so much timber, so many villages concealed in woods or hollows, so many field paths, sunk lanes, dingles, copses, such an unpredictable variety of cottage, farmhouse, villa, and country seat, that the whole thing could never lie clearly in my mind, and to walk in it daily gave one the same sort of pleasure that there is in the labyrinthine complexity of Malory or the *Faerie Queene*… On a Saturday afternoon in winter, when nose and fingers might be pinched enough to give an added relish to the anticipation of tea and fireside, and the whole weekend's reading lay ahead, I suppose I reached as much happiness as is ever to be reached on earth. And especially if there were some new, long-coveted book awaiting me.

≈ *SURPRISED BY JOY*

The way to
the world's end

The country I grew up in had everything to encourage a romantic bent... It is by southern English standards bleak... There is nearly always a wind whistling through the grass. Where you see a man ploughing there will be gulls following him and pecking at the furrow. There are no field paths or rights of way, but that does not matter for everyone knows you... The soil has none of the rich chocolate or ochre you find in parts of England: it is pale... But the grass is soft, rich, and sweet, and the cottages, always whitewashed and single-storeyed and roofed with blue slate, light up the whole landscape...

That is one beauty; and here where you stand is another, quite different and even more dearly loved – sunlight and grass and dew, crowing cocks and gaggling ducks. In between them, on the flat floor of the valley at your feet, a forest of factory chimneys, gantries, and giant cranes rising out of a welter of mist, lies Belfast...

Now step a little way... and you will see a different world. And having seen it, blame me if you can for being a romantic. For here is the thing itself, utterly irresistible, the way to the world's end, the land of longing, the breaking and blessing of hearts.

≈ *SURPRISED BY JOY*

Music – highest of the arts

It must be lovely to really appreciate music... My taste for it was always that of a philistine. Perhaps it is as well I was not with you, or I might just have sat eating my heart out because I couldn't enjoy what I would have enjoyed in those delightful days when we first 'discovered' one another...

Your remarks about music would seem to lead back to my old idea about a face always being a true index of character: for in that case if you imagined from the music of the soul either of Gordon or of this mysterious *fille aux cheveux de lin* one would be bound to imagine the face too

– not of course exactly, but in its general tone. What type of person is this girl of whom Debussy has been talking to you? As to your other suggestions about old composers like Schubert or Beethoven, I imagine that, while modern music expresses both feeling, thought and imagination, they expressed pure feeling. And you know all day sitting at work, eating, walking, etc., you have hundreds of feelings that can't (as you say) be put into words. And that is why I think that in a sense music is the highest of the arts, because it really begins where the others leave off.

Procession of Flora,
ELISABETH SONREL

≈ *THEY STAND*
TOGETHER

Private happiness

The secular community, since it exists for our natural good and not for our supernatural, has no higher end than to facilitate and safeguard the family, and friendship, and solitude. To be happy at home, said Johnson, is the end of all human endeavour. As long as we are thinking only of natural values we must say that the sun looks down on nothing half so good as a household laughing together over a meal, or two friends talking over a pint of beer, or a man alone reading a book that interests him;

C.S. Lewis

and that all economics, politics, laws, armies, and institutions, save in so far as they prolong and multiply such scenes, are a mere ploughing the sand and sowing the ocean, a meaningless vanity and vexation of spirit...

Collective activities are, of course, necessary. Great sacrifices of this private happiness by those who have it may be necessary in order that it may be more widely distributed. All may have to be a little hungry in order

that none may starve. But do not let us mistake necessary evils for good. The mistake is easily made. Fruit has to be tinned if it is to be transported, and has to lose thereby some of its good qualities. But one meets people who have learned actually to prefer the tinned fruit to the fresh. A sick society must think much about politics, as a sick man must think much about his digestion: to ignore the subject may be fatal cowardice for the one as for the other. But if either comes to regard it as the natural food of the mind – if either forgets that we think of such things only in order to be able to think of something else – then what was undertaken for the sake of health has become itself a new and deadly disease...

≈ 'MEMBERSHIP'

A kind of dance

In Christianity God is not a static thing – not even a person – but a dynamic, pulsating activity, a life, almost a kind of drama. Almost, if you will not think me irreverent, a kind of dance. The union between the Father and the Son is such a live concrete thing that this union itself is also a Person... What grows out of the joint life of the Father and Son is a real Person, is in fact the Third of the three Persons who are God... This third Person is called, in technical language, the Holy Ghost or the 'spirit' of God...

And now, what does it all matter? It matters more than anything else in the world. The whole dance, or drama, or pattern of this three-Personal life is to be played out in each one of us: or (putting it the other

way round) each one of us has got to enter that pattern, take his place in the dance. There is no other way to the happiness for which we were made. Good things as well as bad, you know, are caught by a kind of infection. If you want to get warm you must stand near the fire: if you want to be wet you must get into the water. If you want joy, power, peace, eternal life, you must get close to, or even into, the thing that has them. They are not a sort of prize which God could, if He chose, just hand out to anyone. They are a great fountain of energy and beauty spurting up at the very centre of reality. If you are close to it, the spray will wet you: if you are not, you will remain dry. Once a man is united to God, how could he not live for ever?

≈ *MERE CHRISTIANITY*

My Destiny,
VICTOR HUGO (1802–85)

Mirth

'Now let us stint all this and speak of mirth'... At last we can turn to better things. If we think 'mirth' an unsuitable word for them, that may show how badly we need something which the Psalms can give us perhaps better than any other book in the world.

David, we know, danced before the Ark. He danced with such abandon that one of his wives... thought he was making a fool of himself. David didn't care whether he was making a fool of himself or not. He was rejoicing in the Lord...

The most valuable thing the Psalms do for me is to express that same delight in God which made David dance. I am not saying that this is pure or so profound a thing as the love of God reached by the greatest Christian saints and mystics... I am comparing it with the merely dutiful 'churchgoing' and laborious 'saying our prayers'... Against that it stands out as something astonishingly robust, virile, and spontaneous; something we may regard with an innocent envy and may hope to be infected by as we read...

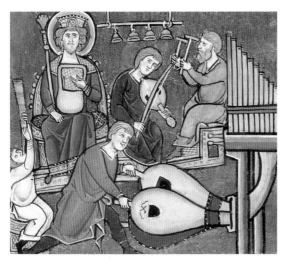

King David and the Psaltery Musicians, from the *Beatae Elisabeth Psalter* (13TH CENTURY)

These old poets do not seem to think that they are meritorious or pious for having such feelings; nor, on the other hand, that they are privileged in being given the grace to have them. They are at once less priggish about it than the worst of us and less humble – one might almost say, less surprised – than the best of us. It has all the cheerful spontaneity of a natural, even a physical, desire. It is gay and jocund… (In the Psalms) I find an experience fully God-centred, asking of God no gift more urgently than His presence, the gift of Himself, joyous to the highest degree, and unmistakably real.

≈ *REFLECTIONS ON THE PSALMS*

The naked Other

I saw that all my waitings and watchings for Joy... had been a futile attempt to contemplate the enjoyed. All that such watching and waiting ever *could* find would be either an image... or a quiver in the diaphragm... These images or sensations... were merely the mental track left by the passage of Joy – not the wave but the wave's imprint on the sand... For all images and sensations, if idolatrously mistaken for Joy itself, soon honestly confessed themselves inadequate. All said, in the last resort, 'It is not I. I am only a reminder. Look! Look! What do I remind you of?'

I perceived (and this was a wonder of wonders) that... I had been equally wrong in supposing that I desired Joy itself. Joy itself, considered simply as an event in my own mind, turned out to be of no value at all. All the value lay in that of which Joy was the desiring... Last of all I had asked if Joy itself was what I wanted; and, labelling it 'aesthetic experience', had pretended I could answer Yes. But that answer too had broken down...

I did not yet ask, Who is the desired? only What is it? But this brought me already into the region of awe, for I thus understood that in deepest solitude there is a road right out of the self, a commerce with something which, by refusing to identify itself with any object of the senses, or anything whereof we have biological or social need, or anything imagined, or any state of our own minds, proclaims itself sheerly objective... The naked Other, imageless (though our imagination salutes it with a hundred images), unknown, undefined, desired.

≈ *SURPRISED BY JOY*

Rapture will not stay

Today was all unlike another day.
The long waves of my sleep near morning broke
On happier beaches, tumbling lighted spray
Of soft dreams filled with promise. As I woke,
Like a huge bird, Joy with the feathery stroke
Of strange wings brushed me over. Sweeter air
Came never from dawn's heart. The misty smoke
Cooled it upon the hills. It touched the lair
Of each wild thing and woke the wet flowers everywhere…

We do not know the language Beauty speaks,
She has no answer to our questioning,
And ease to pain and truth to one who seeks
I know she never brought and cannot bring.
But, if she wakes a moment, we must fling
Doubt at her feet, not answered, yet allayed.
She beats down wisdom suddenly. We cling
Fast to her flying skirts and she will fade,
Even at the kiss of welcome, into deepest shade...

And then I knew that this was all gone over.
I shall not live like this another day.
Tomorrow I'll go wandering, a poor lover
Of earth, rejected, outcast every way,
And see not, hear not. Rapture will not stay
Longer than this, lest mortals grow divine
And old laws change too much. The sensitive ray
Of Beauty, her creative vision fine,
Pass. I am hers, but she will not again be mine.

≈ 'JOY'

This sweet Desire

The experience is one of intense longing. It is distinguished from other longings by two things. In the first place, though the sense of want is acute and even painful, yet the mere wanting is felt to be somehow a delight. Other desires are felt as pleasures only if satisfaction is expected in the near future: hunger is pleasant only while we know (or believe) that we are soon going to eat. But this desire, even when there is no hope of possible satisfaction, continues to be prized, and even to be preferred to anything else in the world, by those who have once felt it. This hunger is better than any other fullness; this poverty better than all other wealth…

In the second place, there is a peculiar mystery about the *object* of this Desire. Inexperienced people (and inattention leaves some inexperienced all their lives) suppose, when they feel it, that they know what they are desiring…

If a man diligently followed this desire, pursuing the false objects until their falsity appeared and then resolutely abandoning them, he must come out at last

into the clear knowledge that the human soul was made to enjoy some object that is never fully given – nay, cannot even be imagined as given – in our present mode of subjective and spatio-temporal experience. This Desire was, in the soul, as the Siege Perilous in Arthur's castle – the chair in which only one could sit. And if nature makes nothing in vain, the One who can sit in this chair must exist.

≈ *PREFACE TO THE PILGRIM'S REGRESS*

The Wanderer over the Sea of Clouds,
CASPAR-DAVID FRIEDRICH (1774–1840)

Creech Hill Fairy, JAMES LYNCH (B.1956)

A tune we
have not heard

In speaking of this desire for our own far-off country, which we find in ourselves even now, I feel a certain shyness. I am almost committing an indecency. I am trying to rip open the inconsolable secret in each one of you – the secret which hurts so much that you take your revenge on it by calling it names like Nostalgia and Romanticism and Adolescence; the secret also which pierces with such sweetness that when, in very intimate conversation, the mention of it becomes imminent, we grow awkward and affect to laugh at ourselves; the secret

we cannot hide and cannot tell, though we desire to do both. We cannot tell it because it is a desire for something that has never actually appeared in our experience. We cannot hide it because our experience is constantly suggesting it, and we betray ourselves like lovers at the mention of a name...

The books or the music in which we thought the beauty was located will betray us if we trust to them; it was not *in* them, it only came *through* them, and what came through them was longing. These things – the beauty, the memory of our own past – are good images of what we really desire; but if they are mistaken for the thing itself they turn into dumb idols, breaking the hearts of their worshippers. For they are not the thing itself; they are only the scent of a flower we have not found, the echo of a tune we have not heard, news from a country we have never yet visited. Do you think I am trying to weave a spell? Perhaps I am; but remember your fairy tales. Spells are used for breaking enchantments as well as for inducing them. And you and I have need of the strongest spell that can be found to wake us from the evil enchantment of worldliness.

≈ 'THE WEIGHT OF GLORY'

Her inmost
spirit shone

S ome kind of procession was approaching us, and the light came from the persons who composed it. First came bright Spirits, not the spirits of men, who danced and scattered flowers – soundlessly falling, lightly drifting flowers, though by the standards of the ghost-world each petal would have weighed a hundredweight, and their fall would have been like the crashing of boulders. Then, on the left and right, at each side of the forest avenue, came youthful shapes, boys upon one hand, and girls upon the other. If I could remember their singing and write down the notes, no man who read that score

would ever grow sick or old. Between them went musicians: and after these a lady in whose honour all this was being done.

I cannot now remember whether she was naked or clothed. If she were naked, then it must have been the almost visible penumbra of her courtesy and joy which produces in my memory the illusion of a great and shining train that followed her across the happy grass. If she were clothed, then the illusion of nakedness is doubt-

less due to the clarity with which her inmost spirit shone through the clothes. For clothes in that country are not a disguise: the spiritual body lives along each thread and turns them into living organs. A robe or a crown is there as much one of the wearer's features as a lip or an eye.

≈ *THE GREAT DIVORCE*

Rising from Sleep in the Morning, STANLEY SPENCER (1891–1959)

Something
super-personal

A world of one dimension would be a straight line. In a two-dimensional world, you still get straight lines, but many lines make one figure. In a three-dimensional world, you still get figures but many figures make one solid body. In other words, as you advance to more real and more complicated levels, you do not leave behind you the things you found on the simpler levels: you still have them, but combined in new ways – in ways you could not imagine if you knew only the simpler levels.

Now the Christian account of God involves just the same principle. The human level is a simple and rather

empty level. On the Divine level you still find personalities; but up there you find them combined in new ways which we, who do not live on that level, cannot imagine. In God's dimension, so to speak, you find a being who is three Persons while remaining one Being, just as a cube is six squares while remaining one cube...

Of course we cannot fully conceive a Being like that... But we can get a faint notion of it. And when we do, we are then, for the first time in our lives, getting some positive idea, however faint, of something super-personal – something more than a person. It is something we could never have guessed, and yet, once we have been told, one almost feels one ought to have been able to guess it because it fits in so well with all the things we know already.

You may ask, 'If we cannot imagine a three-personal Being, what is the good of talking about Him?' Well, there isn't any good talking about Him. The thing that matters is being actually drawn into that three-personal life, and that may begin at any time.

$\approx$ *MERE CHRISTIANITY*

It will be morning

Christ says, 'Give me all. I don't want so much of your time and so much of your money and so much of your work: I want YOU... Hand over the whole natural self, all the desires which you think innocent as well as the ones you think wicked – the whole outfit. I will give you a new self instead. In fact, I will give you Myself: My own will shall become yours.'

Both harder and easier than what we are all trying to do... The real problem of the Christian life comes where people do not normally look for it. It comes the very moment you wake up each morning. All your wishes and hopes for the day rush at you like wild aimals. And the first job each morning consists simply in shoving them all back; in listening to that other voice, taking that other point of view, letting that other larger, stronger, quieter life come flowing in. And so on, all day...

When He said 'Be perfect,' He meant it. He meant that we must go in for the full treatment. It is hard; but the sort of compromise we are all hankering after is harder – in fact, it is impossible. It may be hard for an egg to turn into a bird: it would be a jolly sight harder for it to learn to fly while remaining an egg. We are like

eggs at present. And you cannot go on indefinitely being just an ordinary, decent egg. We must be hatched or go bad...

What we have been told is how we men can be drawn into Christ – can become part of that wonderful present which the young Prince of the universe wants to offer to His Father – that present which is Himself and therefore us in Him. It is the only thing we were made for. And there are strange, exciting hints in the Bible that when we are drawn in, a great many other things in Nature will begin to come right. The bad dream will be over: it will be morning.

≈ *MERE CHRISTIANITY*

It must be great *fun*

The Christian view is precisely that the Next Step has already happened. And it is really new. It is not a change from brainy men to brainier men: it is a change that goes off in a totally different direction – a change from being creatures of God to being sons of God. The first instance arrived in Palestine two thousand years ago. In a sense, the change is not 'Evolution' at all, because it is not something arising out of the natural process of events but something coming into nature from outside…

Already the new men are dotted here and there all over the earth. Some, as I have admitted, are still hardly recognizable: but others can be recognized. Every now and then one meets them. Their very voices and faces are different from ours; stronger, quieter, happier, more radiant. They begin where most of us leave off. They are, I say, recognizable; but you must know what to look for. They will not be very like the idea of 'religious people' which you have formed from your general

The Last Judgement (detail), PETRU RARES (FL.1547)

reading. They do not draw attention to themselves. You tend to think that you are being kind to them when they are really being kind to you. They love you more than other men do, but they need you less... They will usually seem to have a lot of time: you will wonder where it comes from. When you have recognized one of them, you will recognize the next one much more easily. And I strongly suspect (but how should I know?) that they recognize one another immediately and infallibly, across every barrier of colour, sex, class, age, even of creeds. In that way, to become holy is rather like joining a secret society. To put it at the very lowest, it must be great *fun.*

≈ *MERE CHRISTIANITY*

The Vision of St Theresa, JOHN ARMSTRONG (1893–1973)

The resurrection
of the senses

About the resurrection of the body. I agree with you that the old picture of the soul reassuming the corpse – perhaps blown to bits or long since usefully dissipated through nature – is absurd. Nor is it what St Paul's words imply. And I admit that if you ask what I substitute for this, I have only speculations to offer.

The principle behind these speculations is this. We are not, in this doctrine, concerned with matter as such at all: with waves, and atoms and all that. What the soul cries out for is the resurrection of the senses. Even in this

life matter would be nothing to us if it were not the source of sensations…

Don't run away with the idea that when I speak of the resurrection of the body I mean merely that the blessed dead will have excellent memories of their sensuous experiences on earth. I mean it the other way round: that memory as we now know it is a dim foretaste, a mirage even, of a power which the soul, or rather Christ in the soul (He 'went to prepare a place for us') will exercise hereafter. It need not be intermittent. Above all, it need no longer be private to the soul in which it occurs. I can now communicate to you the vanished fields of my boyhood – they are building estates today – only imperfectly by words. Perhaps the day is coming when I can take you for a walk through them.

At present we tend to think of the soul as somehow 'inside' the body. But the glorified body of the resurrection as I conceive it – the sensuous life raised from its death – will be inside the soul. As God is not in space but space is in God.

I have slipped in 'glorified' almost unawares. But this glorification is not only promised, it is already foreshadowed.

≈ *PRAYER: LETTERS TO MALCOLM*

A merry meeting

The Englishness of English is audible only to those who know some other language as well. In the same way and for the same reason, only Supernaturalists really see Nature. You must go a little away from her, and then turn round, and look back. Then at last the true landscape will become visible. You must have tasted, however briefly, the pure water from beyond the world before you can be distinctly conscious of the hot, salty tang of Nature's current. To treat her as God, or as Everything, is to lose the whole pith and pleasure of her. Come out, look back, and then you will see… this astonishing cataract of bears, babies, and bananas: this immoderate deluge of atoms, orchids, oranges, cancers, canaries, fleas, gases, tornadoes and toads. How could you ever have thought this was the ultimate reality? How could you ever have thought that it was merely a stage-set for the moral drama of men and women?

Nature is herself. Offer her neither worship nor contempt. Meet her and know her. If we are immortal,

Earthly Paradise, JAN BRUEGHEL (1568–1625)

and if she is doomed (as the scientists tell us) to run down and die, we shall miss this half-shy and half-flamboyant creature, this ogress, this hoyden, this incorrigible fairy, this dumb witch. But the theologians tell us that she, like ourselves, is to be redeemed. The 'vanity' to which she was subjected was her disease, not her essence. She will be cured, but cured in character: not tamed (Heaven forbid) nor sterilized. We shall still be able to recognize our old enemy, friend, playfellow and foster-mother, so perfected as to be not less, but more, herself. And that will be a merry meeting.

≈ *MIRACLES*

Books in Heaven

'Yes,' my friend said. 'I don't see why there shouldn't be books in Heaven. But you will find that your library in Heaven contains only some of the books you had on earth.'

'Which?' I asked.

'The ones you gave away or lent.'

'I hope the lent ones won't still have all the borrowers' dirty thumb-marks,' said I.

'Oh yes they will,' said he. 'But just as the wounds of the martyrs will have turned into beauties, so you will find that the thumb-marks have turned into beautiful illuminated capitals or exquisite marginal woodcuts.'

Something of God

'The angels,' he said, 'have no senses; their experience is purely intellectual and spiritual. That is why we know something about God which they don't. There are particular aspects of His love and joy which can be communicated to a created being only by sensuous experience. Something of God which the Seraphim can never quite understand flows into us from the blue of the sky, the taste of honey, the delicious embrace of water whether cold or hot, and even from sleep itself.'

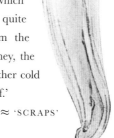

≈ 'SCRAPS'

Huge pleasures

It was early evening when my journey began. The train was full, but not yet uncomfortably so, of people going home… I could not help it – the clicking of all those garden gates, the opening of all those front doors… came over my imagination with all the caress of a half-remembered bit of music. There is an extraordinary charm in other people's domesticities… The pleasure is, once more, the mirror pleasure – the pleasure of seeing as an outsider what is to others an inside, and realizing that you are doing so…

There was the charm, as we went on, of running out into evening sunlight, but still in a deep gulley – as if the train were swimming in earth instead of either sailing on it like a real train or worming beneath it like a real tube. There was the charm of sudden silence at stations I had never heard of, and where we seemed to stop for a long time… But I need not try to enumerate all the ingredients. The point is that all these things between them built up for me a degree of happiness which I must not try to assess because, if I did, you would think I was exaggerating.

Late Summer Landscape, DEROLD PAGE

But wait. 'Built up' is the wrong expression. They did not actually impose this happiness; they offered it. I was free to take it or not as I chose – like distant music which you need not listen to unless you wish, like a delicious faint wind on your face which you can easily ignore. One was invited to surrender to it…

But side by side with this, accompanying it all the way like that ghost compartment which we see through the windows of a train at night, there runs something else. We can ignore it if we choose; but it constantly offers to come in. Huge pleasures, never quite expressible in words…

≈ 'HEDONICS'

The Grace
is not frustrated

How right you are: the great thing is to stop thinking about happiness. Indeed the best thing about happiness itself is that it liberates you from thinking about happiness – as the greatest pleasure that money can give us is to make it unnecessary to think about money. And one sees why we have to be taught the 'not thinking' when we lack as well as when we have. And I'm sure that, as you say, you will 'get through

somehow in the end.' Here is one of the fruits of unhappiness: that it forces us to think of life as something to go *through*. And out at the other end. If only we could steadfastly do that while we are happy, I suppose we should need no misfortunes. It is hard on God really. To how few of us He *dare* send happiness because He knows we will forget Him if He gave us any sort of nice things for the moment…

I *do* get that sudden feeling that the whole thing is hocus pocus and it now worries me hardly at all. Surely the mechanism is quite simple? Sceptical, incredulous, materialistic *ruts* have been deeply engraved in our thought, perhaps even in our physical brains by all our earlier lives. At the slightest jerk our thought will flow down those old ruts. And

Mephistopheles and Marguerite in the Cathedral, FRANK CADOGAN COWPER (1877–1958)

notice when the jerks come. And if you were a devil would you not give the jerk just at those moments? I think that all Christians have found that he is very active near the altar or on the eve of conversion: worldly anxieties, physical discomforts, lascivious fancies, doubt, are often poured in at such junctures... But the Grace is not frustrated. One gets *more* by pressing steadily on through these interruptions than on occasions when all goes smoothly...

≈ *LETTERS OF C.S. LEWIS*

Jephthah's Daughter, GUSTAVE DORÉ (1832–83)

Something outside our experience

Finally we have those instances where poetic language expresses an experience which is not accessible to us in normal life at all, an experience which the poet himself may have imagined and not, in the ordinary sense, 'had'. An instance would be when Asia, in *Prometheus Unbound*, says 'My soul is an enchanted boat'. If anyone thinks this is only a more musical and graceful way of saying, 'Gee! this is fine,' I disagree with

him. An enchanted boat moves without oar or sail to its destined haven. Asia is at that moment undergoing a process of transfiguration, almost of apotheosis. Effortless and unimpeded movement to a goal desired but not yet seen is the point. If we were experiencing Asia's apotheosis we should feel like that. In fact we have never experienced apotheosis. Nor, probably, has Shelley. But to communicate the emotion which would accompany it is to make us know more fully than before what we meant by apotheosis.

This is the most remarkable of the powers of poetic language: to convey to us the quality of experiences which we have not had, or perhaps can never have, to use factors within our experience so that they become pointers to something outside our experience – as two or more roads on a map show us where a town that is off the map must lie. Many of us have never had an experience like that which Wordsworth records near the end of *Prelude 13;* but when he speaks of 'the visionary dreariness' I think we get an inkling of it.

≈ *'THE LANGUAGE OF RELIGION'*

She made beauty
all round her

Of Psyche's beauty – at every age the beauty proper to that age – there is only this to be said, that there were no two opinions about it, from man or woman, once she had been seen. It was beauty that did not astonish you till afterwards when you had gone out of sight of her and reflected on it. While she was with you, you were not astonished. It seemed the most natural thing in the world. As the Fox delighted to say, she was 'according to nature'; what every woman, or even every thing, ought to have been and meant to be, but had missed by some trip of chance. Indeed, when you looked at her you believed, for a moment, that they had not missed it. She made beauty all round her. When she trod on mud, the mud was beautiful; when she ran in the rain, the rain was silver. When she picked up a toad – she had the strangest and, I thought, unchanciest love for all manner of brutes – the toad became beautiful.

The years, doubtless, went round then as now, but in my memory it seems to have been all springs and summers. I think the almonds and the cherries

blossomed earlier in those years and the blossoms lasted longer; how they hung on in such winds I don't know, for I see the boughs always rocking and dancing against blue-and-white skies, and their shadows flowing water-like over all the hills and valleys of Psyche's body. I wanted to be a wife so that I could have been her real mother. I wanted to be a boy so that she could be in love with me. I wanted her to be my full sister instead of my half sister. I wanted her to be a slave so that I could set her free and make her rich.

≈ *TILL WE HAVE FACES*

Cupid and Psyche, EDWARD BURNE-JONES (1833-98)

Acknowledgements

The Editor and Publishers are grateful for permission to use the following
material, which is reproduced by permission of the copyright holders.

*The Letters of C.S. Lewis, Letters to Malcolm, Chiefly on Prayer, Reflections on the
Psalms, Surprised by Joy* and *Till We Have Faces*, and the essay and poem
'Hedonics' and 'Joy' are reproduced by kind permission
of Harcourt Brace & Company.
The Great Divorce, Mere Christianity, Miracles and the essays 'Membership'
and 'The Weight of Glory' are reproduced by kind permission
of HarperCollins*Publishers*.
They Stand Together and the essay 'Scraps' is reproduced by kind
permission of Curtis Brown Ltd.
The Pilgrim's Regress and the essay 'The Language of Religion' are
reproduced by kind permission of Wm. B. Eerdmans Publishing Co.

All items are the copyright of C.S. Lewis Pte Ltd.

Full details of the writings of C.S. Lewis can be found in
C.S. Lewis: A Companion and Guide by Walter Hooper,
published by HarperSanFrancisco in 1996.